CONFLICTS WITHIN

A Journey through Real and Lasting Change

ELTON L. YOUNG

ISBN 979-8-88832-118-8 (paperback)
ISBN 979-8-88832-119-5 (digital)

Christian Faith Publishing
832 Park Avenue
Meadville, PA 16335
www.christianfaithpublishing.com

All Scripture quotations, unless otherwise indicated, are taken from the New King James Version of the Bible.

Printed in the United States of America

CONTENTS

ACKNOWLEDGMENT

To my parents, James Fletcher and Frances Marie Young, who taught me that Christianity is a gift, but discipleship costs something. To my father in the ministry, the late great Dr. Virgil J. Caldwell, who exemplified humility and taught me never to give up on my dreams. To my mentor, the late great Dr. Cameron Madison Alexander, who exemplified the ability to find agreement during times of major disagreement, and my inner circle of closely knit friends (you know who you are). Last but certainly not least, to my deceased wife, Brenda Faye Young, who loved and supported me dearly throughout our marriage, and to my six beautiful daughters—Lekisha, La'Shauna, April, Amanda, Shatoya, and Kay'Lee. Without each of you, and my journey through life as your father and each of you as my children, this book would not be possible. It is to all of you that I dedicate this book with all my love.

What gave birth to writing this book? For me, it's safe to say that this book was born from hurt and pain. Writing this book reminded me of something my seminary professor (Dr. Dana Stoddard) often said: "Christianity is a gift, but discipleship costs something." My commitment to discipleship has cost me many things over the years. I've been divorced and remarried. I've been a single dad who— with the help of my mother and sister—learned to raise my girls to the best of my abilities. I know what it feels like to experience the death of your spouse and then must pick up the pieces of your life and continue forward. The above-listed life experiences were what birthed the writing of this book. I've learned by experience that Christianity is free, and discipleship always costs something.

I wanted to write a book that people can sit down to read and find life experiences that they can relate to in one way or another. I have specialized in conflict resolution and management, taught many grief, loss, and separation courses, and worked as a Christian counselor and senior pastor for several years. My desire with this book was to take some important life lessons that I've learned and taught in many trainings and put those lessons in a book. This book shares important training topics concerning life-application lessons. One of the greatest gifts I can give is to share with wisdom what I've learned from life lessons, and how I apply those lessons in life application.

Proverbs 4:5–7 says,

> Get wisdom! Get understanding.
> Do not forget, nor turn away from the words of
> my mouth.
> Do not forsake her, and she will preserve you;
> Love her, and she will keep you.
> Wisdom is the principal thing; Therefore, get
> wisdom.
> And in all you're getting, get understanding.

To face conflicts honestly, courageously, and victoriously, God must be our primary source for life and life application because it is through him that wisdom and understanding are obtained. You can chart a new course where healthy and productive change is possible and real and experience a sense of renewal in your life's purpose. No longer is it about *just living (just existing)*. Wisdom and understanding bring everything to life. Solomon teaches us that "Wisdom is the principal thing;" which is first in importance and defined in Hebrew as obtaining "good sense and skill." In other words, the more wisdom you obtain, the greater your ability to "get understanding," and with understanding comes, by Hebrew definition, "meaning and solution." A wealth of wisdom helps you find meaning and solutions during the most difficult times, no matter the conflict.

As the author of this book, I hope each reader will learn to properly manage or resolve conflicts by exercising good sense and skill and finding meaning and solutions. I want you to possess the strength and ability to refuse to simply react (driven purely by emotion) to conflict but respond (confidently reply) spiritually and intellectually with meaning and solution (understanding) to every conflict you face. Conflict teaches us to view life experiences in the same manner as God does. How does God view life when it comes to conflict. God's viewpoint can be summarized with three (3) important realities:

1. You will *Face Scrutiny.* That's guaranteed.
2. When it comes to people, you must *Earn Trust.*
3. And when it comes to God, He not only sees your *Limitations in Conflict,* but your *Possibilities to Properly Manage or Resolve them.*

INTRODUCTION

Do you desire constant exposure to a healthy and productive atmosphere that produces real and lasting change, or would you rather be enslaved to a cycle of failed attempts to resolve or manage conflict properly? This book will help you answer this question, along with other questions as well:

1. Whose feet do you sit at when it comes to holistic growth and productivity?
2. Who do you choose to lease space out to in your head and heart?
3. Do the living and working environments you expose yourself to daily fill you with joy and fulfillment or pain and regret?
4. At the end of a busy day, do you feel incarcerated or set free?

Personally, I choose to sit at the feet of Jesus for holistic growth and productivity. I reject unhealthy and unproductive thoughts that constantly seek rental space in my head and heart because unhealthy and unproductive atmospheres stagnate my skill development and spiritual growth and, like a computer virus, aim to destroy my spiritual, mental, emotional, social, environmental, and physical well-being. At the end of my busy day, I choose to enjoy the gift of freedom and reject the restraints of incarceration.

If you constantly feel incarcerated and sincerely desire a holistic lifestyle that brings about real and lasting change, then you are reading the right book. *Conflicts Within* is not just about how; it is a book about a transformative experience that equips you to confront, manage, or resolve conflicts properly and helps you avoid atmospheric conditions that constantly leave you exhausted and filled with pain and regret.

What *life experiences* do you now face that are unproductive, unhealthy, and a constant contributor to the atmospheric conditions you would like to see change? It is so much easier to just blame the person and conditions committed to maintaining an unhealthy atmosphere when the reality is that an evaluation of the people and conditions around you must include an honest assessment of yourself because individual responsibility must always be considered.

Ask yourself, "What wreckage in my life must be cleared? Is it the bitterness of my divorce or the death of my soulmate? Is my debris covered with wrong decisions that led to unintended outcomes? Could my refusal to forgive have done more damage to me than to the person I resent and refuse to set free? Am I still holding on to past betrayals that hinder my ability to express and receive love? In every new relationship, do I bring with me unhealthy emotional baggage and wounds from my past?"

If your wreckage continues to define you, your desire to create and maintain a healthy atmosphere for productive change will be hindered, producing more unanswered questions. Therefore, the process begins by asking "*Why?*"

1. Why can't I reorganize my life and move beyond the devastation of my divorce?
2. Why can't I make the memory of my loved one a motivation instead of a barrier?
3. Why can't I improve the quality of my life and mission of servanthood?
4. Why can't I shift power struggles to cooperative problem-solving?

If your questions are not understood, confronted, properly managed, or resolved, your past will continue to dictate your present and fill your future with many more questions and uncertainties. Instead of managing or mastering conflict, the conflict will manage or master you. Think about the conflicts you've allowed to master or manage you. Ask yourself, "What steps will I take to become a part of the solution rather than remain a part of the problem?"

This book will challenge you to examine *life experiences*, measure *life applications*, and evaluate atmospheric conditions using the proper *life lenses*. These lenses bring your experiences into proper focus by helping you identify your *state of mind* (your mental state currently), *quality of emotions* (your ability to manage your emotions and understand or recognize the emotions of others), and *influence of the Holy Spirit* (the influence, quality, and divine force of an Almighty God). These *life-point strategies* will enhance and empower your ability to create and maintain a healthy atmosphere for real and lasting change. You will replace a lifestyle of constant emotional crisis with tenacity and *self-definition* that fulfill your purpose and determination to succeed by knowing who you are (*my person*), where you stand (*my position*), and to whom you belong (*my provider*).

PART 1

SELF-DEFINITION

If you don't define yourself, someone else will. One of the best and most important ways to manage or resolve *conflicts within* is by first knowing who you are, where you stand, and to whom you belong. I call this *self-identification*.

Self-Identification

What is *self-identification*? It is the God-given ability to know who I am (my *person*), where I stand (*my position*), and to whom I belong (my *provider*). Self-identification is where this book begins because having and maintaining a clear definition of who you are is foundational to managing or resolving the conflicts you face and struggle with daily. It's important to understand that the true nature of self-identification embraces a God-ordained life that is not controlled by the expectations and demands of people, society, and trends. Therefore, facing, resolving, or managing conflicts demands a self-definition that is God-directed and uniquely personal. For example, Paul the apostle, expressed a unique and personal self-definition while writing to the churches in Galatia: "Paul, an apostle (not from men nor through man, but through Jesus Christ and God the Father who raised Him from the dead), and all the brethren who are with me, to the churches of Galatia" (Galatians 1:1–2).

There are two (2) key points to understand about the above scripture. First, you must understand the order in which Paul writes. Second, you must also understand precisely why Paul penned those words. Paul's opening statement is unusual within itself because most of Paul's writings begin with a gracious greeting, but here, it does not. Why? In studying the book of Galatians, you will see that attempts to assassinate Paul's name, character, and relationship to

Christ were in full effect. Therefore, simply greeting those charged with assaulting the core definition of who you are demands a proper response. For Paul, the proper response was to begin his letter with self-identification, making it clear to his readers that he knows who he is (my person), where he stands (my position), and to whom he belongs (my provider). The world did not give it, and the world cannot take it away. That's what I call self-identification. Paul was blessed with the wisdom to respond to and answer his critics by teaching them what it means to possess and practice a healthy self-definition. Fast-forward to today, and I believe the same applies to you. Like Paul, you have been blessed with the God-given ability to achieve self-identification in and through Christ. Believe this: if you don't boldly define yourself, others will (right or wrong). When people attempt to label or falsely define you, like Paul, you must be bold enough to reject false characterizations and old labels that no longer apply to you. You must be bold enough to say, this is who I am.

Self-identification was foundational for Paul, and it is for you, too. How many times has your character been assaulted, and you either ignored it or falsely claimed that it didn't matter? How many times have you been falsely labeled and characterized by others without providing an adequate response? Like Paul, you face mounting pressures, criticisms, and character assassination. To properly face and confront those attacks, you must possess a healthy and sound self-definition: you must know who you are (my person), where you stand (my position), and to whom you belong (my provider).

Dealing with conflicts within begins with and demands a healthy self-definition that is God-directed and uniquely personal. If not, your problems will continue to handle you rather than you handle your problems. Right or wrong, the society you live in will apply its own brand of self-definition upon you if you fail or refuse to define yourself properly.

Conflict is a way of life; we cannot avoid, refuse to face, or just walk away from it. You cannot simply walk away from a bitter divorce and believe there will be no lasting consequences when you fail to resolve or properly manage the conflict. The death of your spouse or significant other cannot be avoided by convincing yourself that such a loss does not profoundly impact your existence and ability to move forward. You cannot simply refuse to face your pain and think that everything is going to be all right. Conflicts that are not handled properly and without a healthy self-definition result in the decimation (murder, destruction, or removal) of ideas and feelings. It prevents agreement, restrains collaborative thinking, and establishes and maintains personal isolation. The reality is that conflicts within are real and can have a lasting impact. So rather than run away or refuse to face the conflicts you are variant toward or in opposition with, self-identification lays the foundation for you to experience real, lasting, and productive change.

If you are ready to restore ideas and feelings and be freed from self-imposed restraints and isolation, I have good news. Your time is now, and it's never too late. If you are sick and tired of being sick and tired, it's never too late. If you have surrendered your brand to others and are now ready to reclaim your mantle, or you are fed up and tired of being pushed around and exhausted from dealing with past baggage that continues to trouble your present or dictates a disastrous future, again, I say, it's never too late. Your time of self-definition has arrived.

The possession and practice of self-identification provide you with the ability to

1. *respond* to your critics,
2. *handle* your conflicts rather than allow conflicts to handle you, and
3. *maintain* your own brand (identity) rather than surrendering your brand (identity) to others.

Self-identification empowers you to respond, handle, and maintain yourself. Such empowerment enables you to confront conflicts within and with others boldly, bravely face the aftershocks of grief, loss, and separation, and gracefully face the bitterness, anger, unforgiveness, and any other life-management challenges you face.

How you define conflict is a matter of perspective. For example, what's the first word that comes to mind when you hear the word *conflict*? I've asked this question many times, and here is a list of general responses I often receive:

fight   *anger*
disagreement   *separation*
unforgiveness   *bitterness*

Yes, conflict is often described with the above-listed words, but what if I told you that conflict is more than fighting, disagreeing, and anger? What if I told you that conflict is not only a fight but an opportunity for peace? It is not just a disagreement but an opportunity to find a compromise. It is not just about anger but how to remain calm. As you read this book, you will be challenged to transform your thinking as you look beyond the negative and see the positive through the renewing of the mind.

Conflict can *mature* us in our faith, *draw* us closer to God and one another in relationships, and *provide* opportunities for healing and reconciliation.

Now it's your turn to quote the words of Paul and replace his name and purpose with your name and purpose.

"Paul, an apostle (not from men nor through men, but through Jesus Christ and God the Father who raised him from the dead),"

How will you define your purpose? Paul defined himself as an apostle. How about you? Are you an overcomer, triumphant leader, physician, therapist, preacher, teacher, attorney, or what? Do you know your purpose? If not now, you will later. As my momma often said, "Just keep on praying and keep on living." God will reveal your purpose, which can be multifaceted to you. If you do know your purpose, I want you to write your name and purpose below:

___________________________, an _________________________.

Remember, the world did not give it, and the world cannot take it away. I hope you are feeling empowered right now because you should. You now can boldly say:

This is who I am.
This is where I stand.
This is to whom I belong.

You can speak to the conflicts that hinder your growth and prosperity. Self-definition is paramount to managing or resolving conflict and serves as the foundation for this book.

PART 2

LIFE EXPERIENCES AND LIFE APPLICATIONS

From experience comes application, and from application, we gain the ability to see life through proper lenses. Chapters 2–5 are going to take you on a life journey. This journey will use biblical and practical concepts and stories to teach life lessons. You will be able to witness the life experiences of others and the applications (skills) they learned to practice because of their experiences. As a result of being battle-tested and scarred by life experiences, you learn better ways to achieve life outcomes that will empower you to see life through the proper *life lenses* and help you understand life from a more focused perspective. *Be empowered by the journey.*

CHAPTER 2

A Healthy Atmosphere for Real and Lasting Change

Chapter one (1) states that self-identification begins with knowing who you are (my person), where you stand (my position), and to whom you belong (my provider). Self-definition of this nature allows us to continue this journey by exploring a healthy atmosphere for real and lasting change.

This chapter focuses on creating or maintaining a healthy atmosphere for real and lasting change, beginning with a definition of *atmosphere*. To avoid becoming too technical, I would like to use a simple description of the word *atmosphere* as described by Global Climate Change (climate.nasa.gov). The atmosphere is the life-sustaining air we breathe, enveloping our planet like a pale blue security blanket, clinging to us by gravity. Without this security blanket (atmosphere), we cannot survive.

To create or maintain a healthy atmosphere for real and lasting change, three (3) important steps must be exercised:

Step One (1): Know the Atmospheric Condition

First, if you are struggling with internal conflicts or in conflict with a particular person or persons, remember that your raised awareness and keen understanding of the atmospheric conditions-surrounding conflicts of any kind empowers your ability to test the temperature in the room. If you cannot read the room properly, your ability to resolve or manage the conflict decreases significantly. Skills for properly reading the room are easier said than done when it comes to theory versus practice, which is why practicing your skills is important and necessary to increase your potential for success in real-time.

Here are a few skills you'll need to develop:

1. Observation

    Pay close attention to your surroundings (people, places, and things). What's their body language? What's their voice tone like? Is the atmosphere tribal, friendly, or a combination of both?

2. Communication management

    Manage your communications by managing your tongue. The best way to manage your tongue is by practicing the 80/20 Rule (80 percent listening, 20 percent talking).

3. Respond, don't react.

    Responding to your observations and communications involves thinking. Reacting to them involves an emotional response. When emotions are solely in charge, that's a recipe for disaster and chaos.

4. Manage the environment.

    Your increased ability to observe, followed by knowing when to talk and when to listen, strengthens your response (thinking) and avoids reactions (unmanaged raw emotions). As a result, you can properly manage the environmental conditions (positive or negative), no matter what they may be.

Conflict at home, at work, or in the community can quickly get out of control when there is a lack of understanding of the atmospheric condition. When emotions are solely in charge, the temptation to *fix things* without regard to current conditions is hard to resist. It often results in making matters worse rather than better.

Nalini Singh said, "Emotion without reason lets people walk all over you; reason without emotion is a mask for cruelty." Knowing the atmospheric conditions empowers you to avoid being taken advantage of and helps you resist practicing a form of cruelty that can make you hurt those you love best.

Step Two (2): Know Your Contribution

Your ability to read the room is just the first step in creating and maintaining a healthy atmosphere for real and lasting change. Step 2 involves knowing your contribution to the atmospheric conditions to which you expose yourself and others.

Earlier, I briefly summarized the atmosphere's important role in our lives today. Without the security blanket (atmosphere) that provides the life-sustaining air we breathe, life on this planet, as we know it, would not be possible. In fact, even today, life as we know it depends on how we take care of the atmosphere in which we live. Contributions made naturally, through human ingenuity, and by other factors are constantly changing (for better or worse) the atmosphere that we depend upon for sustained life. As important as it is to know your contributions to the earth's atmosphere, it is equally important to know your contributions to the atmosphere surrounding the conflict. For example, is the atmosphere healthy and ripe for real and lasting change, or is the atmosphere toxic and resistant to change? The answer to this question depends in part on you. Your thoughts, feelings, behaviors, and actions either contribute toward atmospheric toxicity or the potential for real and lasting change. As the introduction states, what you bring to the table regarding wisdom (good sense and skill) and understanding (meaning and solution) makes a difference.

The opportunity to be the change you wish to see in yourself, and others is available to you. It is vital in how you live and function and in what you expose yourself and others to environmentally. If your contributions to atmospheric conditions are deemed toxic and unproductive, then you need to come clean with God, yourself, and others if you intend to experience a healthy atmosphere for real and lasting change. That means that you must take responsibility for the mistakes you've made. If you don't, then not only are you hindering the possibility of resolving or managing conflict, but you will birth what the mental health community calls *stinking thinking* by feeding into the negative thoughts, feelings, behaviors, and actions that possess you.

Here's what stinking thinking has the power to do:

1. It keeps you focused on your fears and failures.
2. It enslaves you in a cycle of nonproductivity and encourages you to surrender your God-given potential to the enemy.
3. It manufactures one crisis after another.
4. It surfaces barriers and handicaps in your life for the sole purpose of making you feel like you are less than or not enough.
5. It will cause you to repeatedly make the same mistakes and relive the same unproductive history.
6. It will deny you access to peace and real and lasting change.

Where and when appropriate, acknowledge your mistakes by recognizing the problem, refuse to justify the toxic behaviors to which you've exposed yourself and others, and, with good intentions and to the best of your abilities, offer a solution for problems you've created. These actions will play an important role in decreasing your toxicity (stinking thinking) and how much you expose others to.

If the atmosphere is going to change, that change starts with you knowing your contribution. Either your stinking thinking is going to control or manage you, or you are going to control or manage such toxic thinking."

What thoughts and feelings are you struggling with today? How do those thoughts and feelings cause you to behave, and what actions do you take? What can you do right now to help yourself overcome the barriers that are playing out in your heart and mind? Here's part of the answer: Now is a good time to find a secret place to pour your heart and mind out to God as you take ownership of your mistakes and seek God's forgiveness for the toxic and unhealthy atmospheres to which you've exposed yourself and possibly others. Don't think that what I'm encouraging you to do right now will be a one-time event. Quite the contrary, sins will be committed as you continue to experience life, and genuine repentance will be required. It's all part of the journey through real and lasting change.

Maybe you've wronged someone and never sought God's forgiveness. Did you give up on marriage when God told you to hang in there? Did a major disagreement with your son or daughter result in hurt feelings, deep resentments, and unspoken words? Are you still angry at God over the death of your spouse or significant other? Whatever struggles you are experiencing, you need to know and understand that available to you is the ability to resolve or manage them and the opportunity for real and lasting change.

Let's conclude this chapter with the third step for creating a healthy atmosphere for real and lasting change.

Step Three (3): Developing and Working a Healthy Habits Plan

Having a plan is simply not enough. You must be willing to work the plan as well. Remember, either you will work the Plan, or a plan will work you. Exchanging a bad habit for one that's good and productive requires persistence. Remember, on average, it takes approximately sixty-six days for a new behavior to become a routine practice that's fully developed and maintained. Below are ten action steps you must practice to successfully develop what I like to call an HHP (Healthy Habits Plan):

Healthy Habits Plan (HHP)

1. Be real with yourself by evaluating the people, places, and things you expose yourself to.
2. Take ownership of the unhealthy patterns and triggers in your life.

3. Create an inner circle of confidants with whom you can freely share your struggles and receive honesty, encouragement, constructive criticism, and support.

4. Plan specific times daily for prayer, meditation, and study of God's Word.

5. Avoid multitasking when it comes to spending quality time with God. Multitasking is not as productive as it's made out to be. If you have too many irons in the fire, don't be afraid to take some out prayerfully.

6. Replace unhealthy activities with healthy ones.

7. Exercise patience and evaluate your successes and failures. When you fail, don't be afraid to try again.

8. Exercise patience and imagine your future by seeing who you are and what you desire to achieve as a present reality in the making and not a distant dream.

9. Do not isolate yourself and your problems; serve unselfishly by also focusing on the lives and needs of others. You may find answers to your dilemmas by helping others through theirs.

10. Give as God has blessed you to give. Don't be afraid to share your time, finances, and resources with others.

As this chapter concludes, I want to ask you an important question. Are you experiencing real and lasting change, or are you exercising Albert Einstein's definition of insanity? Albert Einstein said, "The definition of insanity is doing the same thing repeatedly but expecting different results." Do you constantly struggle with the same issues and experiencing the same unproductive results? If so, it may be because you expect real and lasting change to come from the toxic thoughts, feelings, behaviors, and actions you practice repeatedly. Doing the same things and expecting different results is contradictory by nature and sets you up for failure with the false belief that you can live a toxic life and expect productive outcomes.

Today, you can begin creating or maintaining a healthy atmosphere for productive change by knowing the atmospheric conditions you expose yourself and others to, your contribution to those conditions, and developing your Healthy Habits Plan.

CHAPTER 3

Manage Yourself

Chapter 1 laid the foundation of self-identification. Chapter 2 built on that foundation with a close look at how people contribute to the atmosphere where they live or function and how those conditions may result in a productive change or ongoing barriers that Albert Einstein's definition of insanity defines. You were challenged to take ownership of your thoughts, feelings, behaviors, and actions, as evidenced by creating and practicing your own Healthy Habits Plan (HHP).

Self-identification in terms of knowing who I am (my person), where I stand (my position), and to whom I belong (my provider), coupled with your ability to be real with God as you establish and practice your own Healthy Habits Plan (HHP), can significantly increase your ability to achieve and maintain self-control, which is why I've entitled Chapter 3 "Manage Yourself." Simply put, managing your emotions will help you manage life events rather than life events managing you.

Webster's Dictionary defines *discipline* as "training that corrects, molds, or perfects." I define *discipline* as "training that develops positive outcomes through self-control." I say that because the word *discipline* comes from the word *disciple*, which means *learner*. Depending upon your approach, discipline (learning) can be a good or bad experience.

As a former director in the field of child development, I was blessed with the opportunity to work with youth of various ages. One of the greatest challenges my team and I faced one summer was with a group of youth, many of whom lacked discipline. As a director, I had to develop a disciplinary system that the youth would buy into and respect. That meant staff would have to buy into that same system as well for the system to be implemented and maintained successfully. As a result, I created the motto "Self-management=Self-control - so manage yourself." Each time a youth would start getting out of control, each staff person's first response to that youth would begin with two words: "Manage yourself."

Incentives were earned and given to those who could manage themselves properly. Up-front consequences were immediately applied when self-management was not achieved. Please understand that we did not incentivize youth by rewarding them for meeting normal expectations. We did not want our *self-management=-self-control* disciplinary system to become nothing more than a bribe. Therefore, the expectation was for each youth to go over and beyond what was normally expected of them. We achieved this by making sure each youth understood what *self-management=self-control* looked like and our expectations of them to work the system rather than allow inappropriate behaviors to work them. With that understanding, we sealed this agreement by having each youth and staff place an ink print of their right hand on a large poster and print or sign their name beneath.

The *self-management=self-control* system worked, and the slogan "Manage yourself" became popular among the youth—so popular that when one youth witnessed the misbehavior of another, the youth that witnessed the event would often say, before staff had the chance, "Manage yourself." The disciplinary system helped us enjoy a successful summer program. The slogan "Manage yourself" went a long way in helping our youth understand that discipline is not a bad thing. Many realized that accomplishing self-control requires discipline (a willingness to learn) and being willing to learn (discipline) requires being in control. Well, the same realization can apply to you. You must develop, implement, and practice a workable plan that will help you properly manage yourself as you deal with life events. The truth of the matter is that life events will handle you, or you will handle life events—events like marriage, divorce, death, separation, substance abuse, alcoholism, retirement, and so much more. The list can go on and on. There are many life events to experience, some good and some bad. Life events require a spiritual and intellectual fortitude committed to gathering the necessary resources and skills to manage or resolve whatever events you have experienced properly or may be experiencing.

Life events are often accompanied by conflicts that are dictated by emotions. With that fact in mind, it's important to understand that dealing with those emotions requires a workable plan that you can buy into, implement, and practice. Achieving this means that your *self-management=self-control* strategy needs to connect to your life event because such a connection helps form a workable plan called *Feelings Are Messengers*, which is a strategy that identifies the feeling, defines the message behind the feeling, and properly diagnoses the need. The *Feelings Are Messengers* plan involves three (3) questions you must ask and answer:

1. What's the feeling?
2. What's the message behind the feeling?
3. What's the need?

If you don't like where you are in life, and you are ready to authorize a strategy that will help you properly interpret and confront life events, the *Feelings Are Messengers* strategy is one you should adopt because this strategy knows the event, properly interprets the message, and correctly diagnoses the need.

Let's begin by placing the *Feelings Are Messengers* strategy in three (3) frames:

Frame 1: Feelings
Frame 2: Messages
Frame 3: Needs

FEELINGS ARE MESSENGERS

FEELING:	MESSAGE:	WHAT I NEED:
FEAR	**There is a threat:** Something might hurt or embarrass me. Something might happen that I can't control.	**Protection:** From being hurt, embarrassed, ashamed, or from things getting out of control.
SADNESS	**There has been a loss:** Losing someone I care about. Losing something I care about or an opportunity that might not come again.	**Comfort and understanding:** For the loss of someone or something very important to me. Hope and encouragement: That more opportunities will come my way.
ANGER	**There has been a violation:** My rights have been violated. My time or space has been violated. My sense of self-worth and trust have been violated.	**Reaffirm or reestablish:** My rights, boundaries, worth, and trust.

HAPPINESS	Everything is okay: I feel confident and competent. I feel appreciated and respected. I feel creative and productive	Opportunities to express my confidence and creativity: In my work, relationships and service to others.

Using the "Feelings Are Messengers" chart enables each person to look beyond anger (violation of boundaries) and identify emotions and needs involved in the conflict. As a result, awareness is raised regarding seeing and identifying how life's developmental stages attach to feelings and self-control.

Normally, in development, infants crawl before they walk, eat soft foods before solid foods, and babble before they develop words. When managing emotions in conflict, similar factors apply in a progressive order and offer opportunities to develop closer relationships and increase empathy through the conflict experience.

For example, if your feeling is *fear, sadness, anger,* or *happiness,* what is the message and the need?

If your *feeling* is *fear,* the *message* is that there's a *threat,* and the *need* is *protection.* The threat may be hurtful, embarrassing, and out of your control. To properly deal with the threat, you need protection—protection from hurt, embarrassment, or shame, and things getting further out of control.

If your *feeling* is *sadness,* the *message* is *loss,* and the *need* is *comfort and encouragement.* The loss may be losing somebody or something you care about or an opportunity that might not come again. To properly deal with the loss, you need comfort for the loss of someone or something very important and encouragement that more opportunities will come your way.

If your *feeling* is *anger,* the *message* is that there's a *violation,* and the *need* is to *reaffirm or reestablish.* The violation may be your rights, time, space, sense of self-worth, or trust that's been violated. To properly deal with the violation, you need your rights, boundaries, self-worth, and trust to be reaffirmed or reestablished.

If your *feeling* is *happiness*, the *message* is that *everything is okay*, and the *need* is an *opportunity to express your confidence and creativity*. You feel confident, competent, appreciated, respected, creative, and productive. You must express this message to others in your work, relationships, or service.

The *Feelings Are Messengers* strategy helps you become resolute in handling life events rather than continuing to allow life events to handle you! This strategy helps you manage the emotions connected to the life event, similar to how the youth in our summer program achieved self-management. Using the Feelings Are Messengers strategy, you can significantly increase your ability to manage your emotions properly.

The *Feelings Are Messengers* strategy helps you look beyond the emotion, identify the message, and understand the need(s).

Think about recent conflicts you've faced and how you dealt with those conflicts in terms of spirit, heart, mind, and emotion. Did you handle the conflict, or did the conflict handle you?

How did you handle it when your best friend's spouse died unexpectedly and at a young age? What did you do when you learned that you were being laid off with no idea as to if/when you would return to work? Did you respond (think things through) or react (with pure emotion) to one of your parents' cancer diagnoses? How did you function after your spouse asked for a divorce?

These are all examples of conflicts you may not be able to resolve, but that doesn't mean those same conflicts cannot be properly managed. You do not have the power to raise your best friend's spouse from the dead, but you do have the ability to stand by your best friend's side to console, lift, and encourage day by day. You cannot force your employer to reinstate your employment, but you can look for another job. You did not go to medical school, nor do you have a cure for cancer. Still, you can take your parent to the doctor, provide love and support throughout their treatment cycle and beyond, be their strength in their time of weakness, and have faith when they are lacking. You can't force your spouse to reconcile, but you can demonstrate your desire for reconciliation. Your response may not resolve the conflict, but even in those cases, you still possess the ability to manage it.

What's the difference between managing and resolving conflict? Resolving conflict finds a solution while managing conflict finds healthy and appropriate ways to function amid an unresolved conflict. Why is that important? It is important because not knowing the difference can result in a lot of wasted time and energy when you find yourself trying to resolve a conflict that's only manageable or trying to manage a conflict that can be resolved. The skills you are now developing will help you know the difference and empower you to resolve or manage the conflict. Skills like:

- *Self-Identification. Knowing My Person – My Position – My Provider (God).*
- *Developing a Healthy Habits Plan (HHP)* for real and lasting change.
- Recognizing that *Self-Management=Self-Control.*
- Understanding *Feelings Are Messengers.*

These skills, along with others, are committed to helping you know the difference between what's resolvable and what's manageable and how to maintain self-control as you continue the work toward developing a healthy atmosphere for real and lasting change.

After reading the first three (3) chapters of this book, you may have concluded that you have dealt with conflicts within and with others in the wrong way or from the wrong perspective. Maybe you've started wrong on many occasions. Well, I have good news for you. Starting wrong is something everyone is guilty of. You may have started wrong, but that doesn't mean you have to end wrong. You are now obtaining information and skills that will help you course correct as you continue to face conflicts within, and with others.

The above tools are available and will help guide your thoughts and conversations as you hit the restart button. Chapter four will further provide guidance by teaching you geographical locations in conflict and how to demonstrate and encourage others to move with you to a place where healing and reconciliation are achieved by all involved in the conflict.

CHAPTER 4

Geographical Locations in Conflict

One of many beautiful things about geography is the ability to move. I came across an anonymous quote that says, "The first step towards getting somewhere is to decide that you are not going to stay where you are." Why is that anonymous quote important when it comes to geographical locations in conflict? It's important because in conflict, people often start out in the wrong location. If you want a different outcome, you've got to make a different move. The benefit of knowing how and when to move will help you identify your location and the location of others in conflict. The goal is to encourage yourself and others to move to a cooperative location where relationships can be strengthened and needs properly met.

Let's illustrate geographical locations in conflict by placing each in its respective frame, along with words that best describe the location.

Let's look at the below diagram as an example:

(What's Your Location?)

Give up (surrender) Wave the white flag. ————————————	Give in (survive) Become invisible. ————————————

Declare war (conflict) Confrontation.	Declare peace (cooperation) Achieve mutual benefits.

Frame 1: Give up or surrender—Wave the white flag.
Frame 2: Give in or survive—Become invisible.
Frame 3: Declare war or conflict—Confrontation.
Frame 4: Declare peace or cooperate—Achieve mutual benefits.

Depending on the nature of the conflict and the motive(s) of those involved, one of the above-listed territories will be used as a starting point.

Frame 1: *Give up* is often used when repetitive conflicts have no resolution or management in sight. This geographical location can result in a person becoming so exhausted that they simply give up (surrender—wave the white flag). This action doesn't mean that the conflict has been resolved; it simply means that the person(s) is tired of fighting and has no interest in further engagement.

Frame 2: *Give in* (survive—become invisible). Persons in this geographical location will often give in when other parties involved in the conflict express a self-centered interest that simply meets their own needs at the expense of others. When there is no genuine effort to meet the mutual needs of all involved in the conflict, people in this territory often become invisible, choosing not to have a voice or any further participation.

Frame 3: Declare war (conflict—confrontation). The geographical location that most people are familiar with and accustomed to. This is where most conflicts geographically begin because anger is an emotion that's readily available and easiest to grab hold of. Therefore, many will begin the conflict by seeing the confrontation as a declaration of war rather than an opportunity for peace.

Frame 4: Declare peace (cooperation—achieve mutual benefits). Recognize conflict as an opportunity for peace rather than a casualty of war.

The reality is that, though peace is the goal, many choose not to start there. People often move to other locations before arriving at a place of peace. Let's be honest; how often does anyone get it right the first time? As stated earlier, starting wrong doesn't mean we have to end wrong. The plus side to geography is you don't have to stay in the same place unless you choose to. You can move from one geographical location to another until you get to where you should and need to be.

A good example can be found in John 4:1–30 (The Woman at the Well). As you read this text, consider Jesus's location and the geographical locations of the Samaritan woman.

A Samaritan Woman Meets Her Messiah

Therefore, when the Lord knew that the Pharisees had heard that Jesus made and baptized more disciples than John (though Jesus Himself did not baptize, but His disciples), He left Judea and departed again to Galilee. But He needed to go through Samaria.

So, He came to the city of Samaria, called Sychar, near the plot of ground that Jacob gave to his son Joseph. Now Jacob's well was there. Jesus, therefore, being wearied from *His* journey, sat thus by the well. It was about the sixth hour.

A woman from Samaria came to draw water. Jesus said to her, "Give Me a drink." For His disciples had gone away into the city to buy food.

Then the woman of Samaria said to Him, *"How is it that You, being a Jew, ask a drink from me, a Samaritan woman?"* For Jews have no dealings with Samaritans.

Jesus answered and said to her, *"If you knew the gift of God, and who it is who says to you, 'Give Me a drink,' you would have asked Him, and He would have given you living water."*

The woman said to Him, "Sir, You have nothing to draw with, and the well is deep. Where, then, do You get that living water? *Are You greater than our father Jacob, who gave us the well and drank from it himself, as well as his sons and his livestock?"*

Jesus answered and said to her, *"Whoever drinks of this water will thirst again, but whoever drinks of the water that I shall give him will never thirst. But the water that I shall give him will become in him a fountain of water springing up into everlasting life."*

The woman said to Him, *"Sir, give me this water, that I may not thirst, nor come here to draw."*

Jesus said to her, *"Go, call your husband, and come here."*

The woman answered and said, "I have no husband."

Jesus said to her, "You have well said, 'I have no husband,' *for you have had five husbands, and the one whom you now have is not your husband; in that you spoke truly."*

The woman said to Him, *"Sir, I perceive that You are a prophet. Our fathers worshipped on this mountain, and you Jews say that in Jerusalem is the place where one ought to worship."*

Jesus said to her, "Woman, believe Me, the hour is coming when you will neither on this mountain nor in Jerusalem, worship the Father. You worship what you do not know; we know what we worship, for salvation is of the Jews. But the hour is coming, and now is when the true worshippers will worship the Father in spirit and truth, for the Father is seeking such to worship Him. God is Spirit, and those who worship Him must worship in spirit and truth."

The woman said to Him, *"I know that Messiah is coming" (who is called Christ).* *"When He comes, He will tell us all things."*

Jesus said to her, *"I who speak to you am He."*

And at this *point,* His disciples came, and they marveled that He talked with a woman, yet no one said, "What do You seek?" or, "Why are You talking with her?"

The woman then left her waterpot, went her way into the city, and said to the men, "Come, see a Man who told me all things that I ever did. Could this be the Christ?" Then they went out of the city and came to Him. (John 4:1–30)

Where is Jesus? And where is the Samaritan woman geographically in this conflict?

The text identifies Jesus's location from start to finish as frame 4: Declare peace. The Samaritan woman immediately declares war. She is ready to fight because Jews have nothing to do with Samaritans, so how dare Jesus ask her for water? Let's look at her moves and how Jesus responds to them.

Samaritan Woman

Verse 9: Declare war (confrontation)
Verses 11 and 12: Declare war (confrontation) Verse 15: Give up (surrender)
Verses 19 and 20: Declare war (confrontation) Verse 25: Declare peace (achieve mutual benefits)
Verses 28 and 29: Declare peace (achieve mutual benefits)

Jesus

Verse 10: Declare peace (achieve mutual benefit)
Verses 13 and 14: Declare peace (achieve mutual benefit)
Verses 16 and 18: Declare peace (achieve mutual benefit)

Jesus's request is made with gentleness and compassion, not in a
spirit of confrontation.
Verses 21–24: Declare peace (achieve mutual benefit)
Verse 26: Declare peace (achieve mutual benefit)

The Samaritan woman geographically located herself in a
place of war or confrontation, but as the conversation continued,
she moved to a place of surrender and finally to a place of peace.
The Samaritan woman had to move three (3) times before getting to
where she needed to be. What does her experience say about yours?
How many times have you failed miserably before finally getting it
right? How many conflicts can you think of right now that you handled wrong? How many words do you wish you could take back?
How many moves have you had to make geographically before getting to where you should have been from the beginning? Everyone
is guilty, so why go through life holding onto the mistakes of the
past? Remember, holding onto a negative past can dictate a disastrous future. For the Samaritan woman, knowing her geographical
location in the conflict and eventually moving to where she needed
to be was a life-changing experience.

Are you ready for your life-changing experience? Maybe you
are going through or have already experienced a devastating divorce.
Could it be that after many years of marriage, God called the love
of your life home to be with Him? Have you, or someone you know
been abused? Do you know anyone that's addicted to physician pre-
scribed medications, or some illegal drug? Did your child, or children become a casualty of war, a victim of gang violence, or a sense-
less mass shooting? If you answered "yes" to what's written, or not
written, I'm sure you wrestle with conflicts within and with others.
I'm certain you've started wrong on more than one occasion, but
now, you are ready for a life-changing experience. God will move
you from where you are to where you need to be. But first, you must
know your geographical location.

George Bernard Shaw so eloquently said, "Progress is impossible without change, and those who cannot change their minds cannot change anything." Your life-changing event may require changing your mind in order to change your geographical location.

CHAPTER 5

Analyze the Elements of the Conflict

Knowing your geographical location must also involve the ability to analyze the elements of the conflict. Analyzing means to study or determine the nature and relationship of the conflict. I would like us to explore three (3) elements or structures of conflict in this chapter. Those elements or structures are power, rights, and interests/needs.

As you determine the geographical location of those in the conflict, you must simultaneously perform two (2) important tasks:

1. Define the above-listed elements or structures of the conflict regarding power, rights, and interests/needs.
2. Understand that it is possible to deal with more than one element or structure within conflict simultaneously.

The above tasks are important because understanding each element's role in the conflict helps determine whether the conflict can be managed or resolved. Let's begin this deep dive by exploring three (3) elements or structures in conflict:

> Power: The capacity to control, exercise authority, or influence the behavior of others or the course of events.

> Rights: Realization or defense of just and lawful
> claims that restore and morally correct legal
> rights in a just and honorable manner.
> Interest or need: A longing desire to achieve a par-
> ticular goal that properly defines the need.

Every conflict has embedded desires to influence, restore, and define. Through your analysis, you must determine how those elements shape the conflict you are engaged in. Let's do so by examining historical and current events in the context of the above elements. For example, the institution of slavery can be defined as an element of *power* for the slave owner because this unjust and immoral practice provided a person or group the capacity to control, exercise authority over, or influence the behavior of others with or without consent.

Civil rights can be defined as an element of rights, as evidenced by its ability to legally restore the rights of those discriminated against and morally correct injustices in a just and honorable manner. The desire to be heard—my story—can be defined as an element of interest/need, as evidenced by movements that include but are not limited to the MeToo Movement, Black Lives Matter, Women's Rights, Civil Rights, Environmental Justice, and more. These movements identify the long-desired goal of being listened to and heard.

At the beginning of this chapter, I asked if more than one element could occur within the same conflict. I answered that question by saying *yes*. Under elements of conflict, the above-listed examples and others like them can take place independently or simultaneously. The fact is that we can look through the historical portals of religion, politics, family, and life, in general, and see numerous life events characterized by power, rights, and interests/needs—events that were just, unjust, comprehensible, incomprehensible, moral, and immoral, but, practiced. In fact, today, we continue to struggle with and fight against ghosts from historical footprints of the past. Let's look at some of those footprints using the below-listed elements:

Power

1. *Domestic violence*

   Domestic violence is all about *control*! One person can enforce their will upon another with or without consent.
2. *Sexual abuse*

   A matter of *force*! The exercising of *power*! The perpetrator's ability to take advantage of the vulnerabilities of another person, be it male or female.

Rights

1. Slavery
2. Jim Crow laws
3. Civil Rights (Voting rights—*Brown vs. the Board of Education*, etc.)

Interest/Need

1. Women's Rights
2. Civil Rights
3. The MeToo Movement
4. Black Lives Matter
5. Environmental Justice
6. Equal Pay
7. The Poor People's Campaign

Listing examples could go on and on. Regardless of the element, the ability to resolve or properly manage conflict must involve the skill to identify geographical locations in conflict and the wisdom, knowledge, and understanding to properly analyze the elements or structures (power, rights, and interest) of the conflict.

PART 3

STATE OF HEART, MIND AND EMOTIONS

What was your state of heart, mind, and emotions before you picked up this book and began reading it? Which life struggle were you combating? Anger? Bitterness? Unforgiveness? Failure? Unresolved conflict? Think about where you were then and consider where you are now. In these final chapters, you will complete your exploration of resolving or managing conflict. You will know and understand your mental and emotional state as you recognize the emotions of others and actively engage in each level of conflict.

CHAPTER 6

Rules of Engagement

The military defines rules of engagement as "the internal rules or directives among military forces that define the circumstances, conditions, degree, and manner in which the use of force, or actions which might be construed as provocative, may be applied." Rules of engagement are something I know well because of my service in the United States Marine Corps. As a result of my military training, I understood that before engaging in a conflict, the soldier must clearly understand what they can and cannot do when it comes to confrontation. Let's apply that analogy to conflict management and conflict resolution by further exercising the knowledge you've thus far gained from reading this book and connecting that knowledge to practical skills for proper engagement. It is not by accident that this book's first five (5) chapters deal primarily with self-examination. Foundationally, Chapters 1–5 help you recognize, relate to, and reassess ways to properly examine and define yourself as you confront conflicts within and with others. Thus far, you have taken a deep dive into understanding yourself and your relationship with God, realizing that both relationships significantly influence and define your level and style of engagement when it comes to conflict.

It is my hope that the first five (5) chapters of this book have motivated you towards change where needed and necessary. "If you always do what you always did, you will always get what you always got." *Albert Einstein*

Let's do a summary of the first five chapters:

Chapter 1 Self-Identification: The God-given ability to know who you are, where you stand, and to whom you belong.

Chapter 2 A Healthy Atmosphere for Real and Lasting Change: Rejecting a lifestyle of stagnation and refusing constant exposure to unhealthy atmospheric conditions surrounding people, places, and circumstances.

Chapter 3 Manage Yourself: Your decision to properly manage life events rather than allowing life events to manage you constantly.

Chapter 4 Geographical Locations in Conflict: The importance of knowing your location and the location of others. Where do you reside geographically? Do you surrender, survive, fight, or cooperate?

Chapter 5 Analyze the Elements of Conflict: Understanding that the elements of conflict are identified in the form of power, rights, and interest/need. All of which can be experienced separately and at the same time.

Now that a solid foundation has been laid, you are ready to learn an array of additional skills that you must commit to exercising to achieve further development. Self-identification/self-definition has been achieved and serve as your rulebook for engagement. You can bridge who you are, where you stand, and to whom you belong with King Solomon's words, "Wisdom is the principal thing." You are ready to connect the principal things (good sense and skill) to understanding (meaning and solution) as you battle those conflicts within and with others.

The comprehensive nature of conflict exposes each surrendered person to the fact that conflict is not just about you; it is about your relationship with God and your involvement with others. Therefore, conflict cannot solely be about your needs; it must include recognition and respect for the needs of others.

If your attempt to manage or resolve conflict only recognizes your needs and repeatedly fails to recognize the needs of others, your approach to conflict will continue to be unhealthy, unproductive, and unsuccessful, which is why this book starts with self-examination instead of basic skills for managing and resolving conflict. In this book, the spiritual is placed before the practical because a healthy relationship with God is the gateway to a healthy relationship with humanity. It is the best path to managing or resolving the problems life throws your way.

Are you ready to engage persons or situations you're in conflict with using a well-thought-out and executed plan that will help you properly define facts and issues, successfully explore gateways to problem-solving, create win/win situations, secure commitments, and produce real and lasting change? If your answer is *yes*, you will obtain and develop additional skill sets as you continue to read this book:

- Initiate interactions.
- Clarify, prioritize, reframe, and bridge issues.
- Gateway to brainstorming.
- Achieving resolution or management of the conflict

Let's continue to develop your skills by learning to establish interactions.

CHAPTER 7

Initiate Interactions

Thus far, this book has taught and challenged you to:

1. know who you are
2. avoid, reject, and challenge unhealthy atmospheric conditions where or when possible
3. properly manage life events rather than allow life events to manage you
4. know the geographical locations of yourself and others in conflict, and
5. examine methodically the elements of the conflict.

You are now prepared for the next phase of the conflict management and resolution process—initiating interactions. To *initiate* simply means to begin a process or action. Now that you are ready to act, you must commit to *four guiding principles* of morally acceptable rules for proper conduct. These principles will play a vital role in helping you successfully manage or resolve conflict:

Guiding Principle 1

Integrity and honesty

"The quality or state of being truthful; not deceptive."

Patrick Spencer Johnson said it best, "Integrity is telling myself the truth. And honesty is telling the truth to other people." First, be honest with yourself. Second, be honest with others.

Guiding Principle 2

Respect

"Due regard for the feelings, wishes, rights, or traditions of others."

Respect teaches us that conflict isn't just about you and your feelings. *Respect* teaches you to respect the feelings of others by listening to what others have to say as their feelings, wishes, rights, and traditions are expressed.

Guiding Principle 3

Responsibility

"Answerable or accountable for something within one's power, control, or management."

Accept that you can be part of the cause and the solution for the conflict you face.

Guiding Principle 4

Persistence

"To persist in an idea, purpose or task despite obstacles."

Fear should not be your option because fear is a barricade and hindrance to developing ideas, purpose, or tasks that can help resolve or manage conflict. Therefore, you must continue forward, even when fearful and uncertain of the outcome. There is a greater failure in not trying at all.

Now that four guiding principles have been established, let's take another step in the initiation process by understanding and practicing important dos and don'ts when it comes to initiating interactions:

Do's

1. Work together.
    A general commitment to work together to the best of each person's ability by recognizing each person involved in the conflict as an empowered partner.
2. Practice confidentiality.
    Respect and clearly understand that the role confidentiality plays in this process is, in most cases, voluntary. Understand both the definition and exception(s) that apply.
3. Choose your battles wisely.
    Remember, larger issues can quickly influence and escalate conflict. Therefore, finding areas of commonality first is not only tactful but helps avoid temper tantrums as well.
4. Understand the atmospheric conditions.
    Remember, you will either be exposed to a casual or formal atmosphere. Formal processes often require written agreements and signatures, while casual processes will not require the same. Exercising a formal process under casual conditions or a casual process under formal conditions can be counterproductive and confusing.
5. Maintain a level playing field by being sensitive to all barriers that may interfere with establishing healthy and appropriate interactions.
6. Face-to-face interactions are key to reading body language, providing the best approach for initiating healthy and productive interactions, and managing or resolving conflict.
7. Practice the 80/20 rule by making active listening your primary objective. The balance you want to achieve is 80 percent listening and 20 percent talking.

8. Focus on facts over emotions as you reinforce positives by learning to disagree without being disagreeable.
9. One person speaks at a time as you recognize and acknowledge past mistakes and agree not to dwell on them in a way that will hinder any effort to manage or resolve conflict.
10. Take the necessary pauses or brakes where or when necessary.

Don'ts

1. Don't violate trust by failing to understand that confidentiality can be defined differently when it comes to an individual or group.
2. Don't depend on email, text, Snapchat, Twitter, and other social media platforms to establish healthy and productive interactions. It's nearly impossible to understand voice tones and visualize body language using a platform that does not provide appropriate access for interaction.
3. Don't engage in personal insults and character assassination.
4. Don't point your fingers at each other.
5. Don't talk at each other; talk to each other.
6. Don't prioritize being right over resolving or managing conflict. Remember, resolving or managing conflict is about healing relationships, not about whose right or wrong.

Let's conclude this chapter with two (2) powerful quotes written by psychiatrist and author Scott Peck. Peck said:

> "Human interaction is the key force in overcoming resistance and speeding change."

> "All human interactions are opportunities either to learn or to teach."

How you choose to interact with others during a time of conflict has the potential to remove barriers and bring about change while teaching you vital life lessons at the same time. If I had to choose between experiencing a human or digital connection with another person, my constant desire for human connectivity would win every time because there is so much more to be gained physically, mentally, socially, emotionally, environmentally, and spiritually.

CHAPTER 8

Clarifying, Prioritizing, Reframing, and Bridging Issues

Each interaction in conflict allows you to exercise important strategies you've thus far learned. Strategies like working together, maintaining a level playing field, taking the necessary pauses, practicing the 80/20 rule, and more. Think about it for a moment. Now that you know how to interact, your next step is to learn to talk through those interactions by clarifying issues as they arise.

The message must be clarified to understand the issues. This involves listening and communication skills that help develop the big picture. Let's begin developing the big picture by viewing the issues from the balcony. For example, people often prefer viewing operas, concerts, plays, and other live events from the balcony because it allows an unobscured view of the center stage environment. Issues in conflict serve as the center stage environment. When viewed from the balcony, greater opportunities for resolution or management exist.

What does it mean to clarify an issue? It means to "make (a statement or situation) less confused and more clearly comprehensible." American educator, author, businessman, and keynote speaker Stephen R. Covey once said, "Most people do not listen with the intent to understand; they listen with the intent to reply." If your desire is to lessen the confusion and increase comprehension in conflict, then you must listen to understand before you reply. The ability to listen more and talk less allows the other person to tell their story without interruption. It enables each person involved in the conflict to focus on needs identified through the positional statements each person makes. As a result, the opportunity to prioritize and reframe issues is made available.

Prioritizing Issues

Prioritizing issues can be determined and measured by how well those interactions are going between those in conflict. For example, if trust is established and communications are flowing reasonably well, an opportunity to work on more difficult issues first may be available. But if there is apparent skepticism or resistance, it often helps to start with a readily solvable problem first to build trust in each other and the process. If this is the case, dealing with bigger issues first may be delayed to address smaller details. My father often said, "Trust is something you earn, not something you simply give away." You may have to start with smaller issues before tackling larger ones to earn that trust.

As issues are prioritized and addressed, it's important to understand that some may not be resolved or managed within one visit. If not, assurances need to be made so that every effort will be made to resolve or manage them over an agreed-upon period of time.

Reframing Issues

You are now ready to reframe issues. This process begins by first understanding that there are five ways to frame or express a conflict: as a *position*, as an *interest* (need), as a *preliminary question (PQ)*, *Problem-Solving Question (PSQ)*, and as an *underline need(s)*. A *position* is a demand for a specific way to meet a need. *Interest* can be defined as a general need to be satisfied in one or more ways. A *preliminary question (PQ)* serves as a bridge to the *Problem-Solving Question (PSQ)*, which serves as the gateway to brainstorming, and the *underline need(s)* addresses the core motivating factor(s) behind the issue(s).

Reframing issues is an important skill because it provides an opportunity to identify and connect the position and interest (need) to the preliminary question (PQ) and Problem-Solving Question (PSQ). These connections provide a clearer view of what is happening during the conflict as you test your ideas and determine the direction you desire to take to manage or resolve the conflict.

Let's explore some examples of reframing issues that can be built upon:

Example 1

- Position (a demand for a specific way)
  "No way am I going to school tomorrow!"
- Preliminary question (PQ)
  "Why don't you want to go to school?"
- Interest (a general need to be satisfied)
  "Ray won't leave me alone and keeps talking about me."
- Problem-Solving Question (PSQ) (connect position and interest in the form of a PSQ.
  "How do we help you feel good/safe about attending school and have Ray leave you alone?"

"Is the child experiencing *fear*? Is the child experiencing *anger*? What's your conclusion? Revisit the *Feelings Are Messengers* chart *(pages 17–18)* and make your own determination. Remember, whatever the feeling is, there's a message and need behind it. Incorporating the *Feelings Are Messengers* chart as issues are prioritized, reframed, and bridged makes a powerful combination. Let's look at two (2) more examples."

Example 2

- Position (a demand for a specific way)
  "I am sick and tired of these bills. I can't get ahead because of them."
- Preliminary Question (PQ)

- "Which bills are holding you back?"
- Interest (a general need to be satisfied)
    "These student loans are killing me."
- Problem-Solving Question (PSQ) Connects the position and the interest in the form of a Problem-Solving Question (PSQ)
    "How do we make financial progress while getting your student loans paid at the same time?"

Is the adult experiencing *fear, sadness, anger, or happiness*? Again, review the *Feelings Are Messengers chart (pages 17–18)* and come to your own conclusion. If the feeling is *anger*, the message is that there is a *violation*, and the need is *to reaffirm or reestablish*.

Let's explore one more example:

Example 3

- Position (a demand for a specific way)
    "I do not like how you treat your kids when compared to mine."
- Preliminary question (PQ)
    "How do I treat my kids differently than yours?"
- Interest (a general need to be satisfied)
    "I need you to be fair with the children so one doesn't feel less valued than the other. Christine and Kelly both need new clothes."
- Problem-Solving Question (PSQ) (connect position and interest in the form of a PSQ.

    "I'm sorry. I wasn't thinking. How can I restore
    your trust in my decision-making while ensuring
    Kelly and Christine both have what they need."

Is the parent (mother) experiencing anger? If so, the *message* is that there is a *violation*, and the *need* is to *reaffirm or reestablish*.

It's important to remember that the primary function of the Problem-Solving Question (PSQ) is to open the door to brainstorming. Your ability to connect the position (a demand for a certain way) to the Interest/Need (a general need to be satisfied) using the Feelings Are Messengers chart as your guide can help you generate a response (thoughtful dialogue) rather than a reaction (pure emotion) when it comes to conflicts within, and with others. Don't be surprised, and do not consider it a hindrance when dealing with a conflict that can fit more than one message from the Feelings Are Messengers chart. Remember, there's no limitation on how many problem-solving questions (PSQ) you can ask. Your aim is to find and present the question that will help open the door to brainstorming.

One way to improve your ability to reframe issues is by conducting a Reframing Relay. A Reframing Relay is an exercise that two of my former partners and I developed and made a central part of our conflict training. We would place several large sheets of easel paper on the wall in the classroom. Each easel sheet would list in the following order the below-listed words:

Problem: A different problem would be written
out at the top of each easel page. We would
periodically allow the students to create
their own problem scenarios occasionally.
Position Interest (need)
Preliminary question (PQ)
Problem-solving quest (PSQ)

The first student in the relay would read the problem and write out a position based on the student's interpretation of the problem. The next student in the relay will determine the possible interest (need) based on what's been listed as the position. The next student in the relay will create a preliminary question (PQ) and Problem-Solving Question (PSQ). You can imagine how much fun we would have with this exercise. We enjoyed the flexibility of having the students do the exercise as one group, dividing the student body into groups, and making the process a little more competitive. Either way worked perfectly always resulting in the classroom wall being covered with ideas that would help each student increase their skills while, at the same time, bouncing ideas off one another.

Here's a diagram of the Reframing Relay:

Reframing Relay

Position	Interest/Need	Preliminary Question	Problem-Solving Question

The Reframing Relay helps develop reframing skills. A successful reframing of issues can further develop trust and open the door to exposing the underline need(s) or core motivating factor(s) (CMF). Once that door is open, the opportunity to deal with a deeper level of injury, pain, and trauma may be identified. This doesn't mean that everything will be resolved or properly managed all at once. It does mean that the opportunity for healing is available. Additional mental health resources may be necessary to manage or resolve those issues properly. One of the best ways to better understand the underline needs or core motivating factor(s) is by increasing your knowledge about the developmental stages of humans. The developmental transition a person experiences should always factor into your resolution and management skills.

The ability to identify certain factors may often depend on how well you know the person(s) you're in conflict with. You may not know anything about the person or know a great deal. When it comes to Core Motivating Factors/Underlying Needs, the more you know about the person, the better, because past traumas, life experiences that have not yet healed, and remain exposed along with experiences met throughout life's developmental stages from the cradle to the grave all influence our approach to, and how we deal with conflict. For the above and other reasons not mentioned in this book, I determined that it's important to include a summary layout of developmental stages.

Let's explore stages of development using the below chart:

Developmental Transitions (from the Cradle to the Grave)

Infants (0–18 months)

Mentality: Developing a sense of trust in the environment and primary caregiver.

Characteristics: The infant will identify the environment as loving, warm, and nurturing or as hostile and painful. These senses are made available through the primary caregiver. Excessive crying can signal that something is wrong. The best response is consistent age-appropriate nurturing.

Stress signals: Crying and lack of eating can be signals of stress. This type of stress can result from the child's daily needs not being met and lengthy separation from the primary caregiver.

Proactive response or intervention: Parenting education. Understanding and practicing primary responsibilities of parental and primary caregiving. Consistent prayer, seeking wisdom, knowledge, and understanding to meet the needs of the child while promptly and consistently being sensitive to and avoiding lengthy separations from the infant.

Toddlers (18 months–2 years)

Mentality: Toddlers begin to develop a sense of self as separate from significant others and the environment.

Characteristics: Keeping consistent routines with this age group is important. Toddlers tend to be self-centered and believe that the actions of others directly relate to their actions. They do not cope well with numerous changes in routine. They fear abandonment and need nurturing and warmth from their parents and caregivers.

Stress signals: Fear, irritability, anxiety, and clinging are stress factors in this age group. Fear of separation or abandonment is displayed in crying, clinging, or asking for an absent parent or caregiver. Regression can also take place in this age group.

Proactive response or intervention: Parenting education and consistent routines are crucial for this age group. Some regression is to be expected within this age group. The parent or primary caregiver needs to monitor separation periods closely, remain consistent in prayer, and seek wisdom, knowledge, and understanding as you promptly and consistently meet the child's needs.

Preschool Children (3–5 years of age)

Mentality: Learning their place within the family.

Characteristics: Fantasyland thinking. Act out the role of adults and believe that they control the actions of others by their behavior. Children in this age group can be very self-centered and fear abandonment.

Stress signals: This age group easily projects family problems upon themselves. Fear of the unknown can result in irritable behavior, fear of separation, and regression to earlier childhood behaviors.

Proactive response or intervention: Reassuring this age group with positive words and acts of love is very important. Role-play activities to explain developmental events to this age group and maintaining consistent routines are vital to development as you pray and seek wisdom, knowledge, and understanding as a parent or caregiver.

School Age Children (6–12 Years of Age)

Mentality: This age group needs to achieve a sense of self-worth as skills are further developed.

Characteristics: There is little room for shades of gray and room for compromise with this age group. This developmental period is the age of absolutes, e.g., black, or white and right or wrong. Comfort zones for this age group start to expand beyond the immediate family as their ability to empathize with others increases. This age group generally starts to identify and attach to the same-sex parent. At the same time, they expand and develop new social skills and interest in physical activities.

Stress signals: This age group can feel their parent's pain deeply and can exhibit anger and place blame upon their parent/caregiver. This age group can struggle with identity as they transition into educational/school environments and build social networks among same-age peer groups.

Proactive response or intervention: Communicate clearly to this age group by explaining what's happening and what will occur next, as routines are kept consistent. It is important to inform educators of any stress this age group may be experiencing. Positive role models are important within the family unit as you consistently pray and seek wisdom, knowledge, and understanding as a parent and caregiver.

Adolescents (13–17 years of age)

Mentality: This age group needs to establish an identity separate from the parent or caregiver.

Characteristics: This age group establishes independence as they move away from family. Their rejection of family traditions and other activities often reveals a combination of dependent and independent struggles. Peer approval is important to this age group, and their immediate future is of great concern.

Stress signals: Conflicts between parents can be a major stressor for this age group. Such stress forces this age group to increase their ambivalence as they struggle with deciding to whom to be loyal. This can leave this age group emotionally torn between parents or caregivers. This age group begins to question relationships in terms of marriage and can experience shame, denial, withdrawal, or depression.

Proactive response or intervention: It is important to clearly communicate what's happening to this age group developmentally and how their development affects them and others. This age group needs flexibility, and to avoid being too restrictive with expectations and responsibilities is important. Clearly clarify expectations and limitations to this age group as you allow them to experience more freedom and choice. Take advantage of professional resources as you consistently pray and seek wisdom, knowledge, and understanding as a parent or caregiver.

Young Adulthood (18–24 years of age)

Mentality: This age group transitions from adolescence to adulthood by exhibiting a different style of living in language, appearance, and attitude.

Characteristics: Permanently leaving home, completing higher education, becoming self-supportive, selecting a mate, and attitudes toward religion are important to this age group. Their development involves skepticism, searching, and liberation.

Stress signals: Fear of not achieving a healthy and productive self-definition is significant to this age group. Who am I? What kind of person ought I to be? Self-definition statements and questions of this nature are of vital importance. If not properly answered, this age group often feels trapped in an atmosphere where relationships and life have no valued meaning.

Proactive response or intervention: It is important to create a healthy and respectful atmosphere where differences of opinion are allowed and taken seriously. This age group thrives in environments where self-expression and self-identification are experienced as the parent or caregiver consistently prays and seeks wisdom and understanding.

Adulthood (25–39 Years of Age)

Mentality: This age group identifies with intellectual concerns while in pursuit of more knowledge, healthy social climates, marriage, family, and civil affairs.

Characteristics: Developing fundamental beliefs regarding life and achieving interpersonal satisfaction and contentment with others are characteristics of this age group.

Stress signals: Identity crisis fears and the inability to identify with others intimately and socially are stress signals for this age group.

Proactive response or intervention: The parent or caregiver must learn to balance the need for loving support with tough love as this age group works through personal problems in their own way. The wisdom, knowledge, and understanding you gain in this area as a parent or caregiver will play a vital role in your response or intervention.

Middle Adulthood (40–65 Years of Age)

Mentality: A time when accomplishments are measured by responsibility, accountability, and adjustment.

Characteristics: This age group is characterized by intellectual, social, and biological identification. Achieving balance is important for this age group.

Stress signals: Fear of decline in intellectual, social, and biological abilities commonly rooted in myths and fables are stress signals for this age group.

Proactive response or intervention: Provide instruction and guidance with life issues and transitions adults in this age group struggle with. It is important to encourage participation in recreational and social activities for this age group as each parent or caregiver prays consistently and seeks godly wisdom, knowledge, and understanding.

Senior Adults (66 Years of Age and Older)

Mentality: A time of fulfillment, purpose, and joy.

Characteristics: Making the environment as productive, beautiful, and comfortable as possible allows this age group to use their life experiences to educate, empower, and protect other age groups by sharing their experiences.

Stress signals: Fear of being abandoned, identity crisis fears, and the inability to identify with others intimately and socially are stress signals for this age group.

Proactive response or intervention: Provide information that inspires and informs as you holistically minister to the physical, social, emotional, environmental, intellectual, and spiritual needs of this age group. Pray consistently as God blesses you with wisdom, knowledge, and understanding.

It is important to understand that stages of development are not as automatic as a person's birthday. Being a certain age does not guarantee that you've experienced the developmental characteristics of the corresponding age. Life teaches us that unresolved and unmanaged conflict can lead to developmental stages of regression and potentially return a person to an earlier developmental stage that does not complement their numeric age. In addition, people can choose to regress to a developmental stage where they once felt safe and protected. This can result in failure to experience an age-appropriate developmental stage. For these reasons, among many others, a person's stage of development can and often will play a significant role in identifying Core Motivating Factors (CMF)/Underlying needs as you work to manage or resolve conflict properly.

Throughout my career, I've witnessed how powerful it can be to understand where a person is developmentally when dealing with conflict. It's important to make sure that you don't make the mistake of assuming that the numeric age of a person automatically qualifies them for the developmental stage they should represent based upon their age. Such assumptions would be a mistake because it is not the numeric age that adequately identifies where a person is in their development. It is their level of maturity or lack thereof that does.

Simply put, a forty-year-old person can be stuck in the developmental stages of an adolescent. A person may have been traumatized in such a way that caused them to skip a developmental stage, or they were so overly protected that the opportunity to experience said stage was denied. Where a person is in their development is directly connected in one way or another to Core Motivating Factors (CMF)/ Underlying needs. There is no guarantee that such factors will manage or resolve the conflict, but having such knowledge can greatly assist you with understanding that there's more to the conflict than the current issues at hand and that further exploration through other mental health resources may need to be further explored when appropriate to do so.

In summary, you now know that Feelings Are Messengers and Geographical Locations in conflict are crucial to determining location and destination. In addition, you understand that it is important to know the nature of conflict in terms of Power, Rights, and Interests as issues in conflict are reframed using the Problem-Solving Question (PSQ) to eventually open the gateway to brainstorming, which is what you are about to explore in Chapter 9.

Gateway to Brainstorming: Prelude to an Agreement

The skills you have developed led you to this moment. Practicing these skills will continue to educate, empower, and expand your creativity and knowledge when finding and asking the Problem-Solving Question (PSQ) that opens the door to brainstorming. Brainstorming produces ideas that improve opportunities for proper management or resolution of conflict. The more spontaneous people are in creating ideas, the more creative people become in problem-solving techniques that positively contribute to managing or resolving conflict.

Here are a few formal guidelines that have proven to be helpful during the brainstorming process:

1. When and where appropriate, record ideas as much as possible.
2. Think of and consider different ways to solve the problem.
3. Don't judge or throw out any ideas at first glance.
4. Encourage off-the-wall or outside-the-box ideas and solutions. (Remember, you will consider or judge the effectiveness of those ideas later.)
5. Empower each person to record their ideas.
6. Make sure all ideas are visible and clearly documented for everyone to view.

7. Offer encouragement, support, and positive feedback throughout the brainstorming process.

After all ideas have been generated, each person can use a chart to identify acceptable or workable ideas and rule out other ideas that are not acceptable or workable. Important questions to answer during this exploration of ideas are the following: (1) Does the idea help manage or solve the problem? and (2) Will the idea work? (see Brainstorming Exercise)

BRAINSTORMING	**VOTING**	
Write down all ideas here:	**Likes it**	**Don't Like**

After all ideas have been generated, each person needs to place a check in the columns next to the ideas each person likes or don't like.

TEST SOLUTIONS

The following questions will help determine whether the agreed-upon ideas will work as a possible solution:

1. Does it solve or help manage the problem?
2. Will it work?
3. Does it follow the guidelines of the home, school, etc.?
4. Are we willing to carry the ideas out?
5. Will we be able to tell if it works?

In the grid below, make a list of brainstorming ideas that all parties like.

Brainstorming ideas all parties like:	Checkmark each question answered.					
	1	2	3	4	5	

Brainstorming helps set the terms for effective guidelines, which can lead to an effective agreement. Below is a list of important items you will need to cover within your agreement:

1. Make sure the agreement is signed or verbally committed to.
2. Make sure the agreement is tested by evaluating progress or barriers within fourteen to thirty days.
3. Make sure everyone has a copy of the agreement.
4. Be willing to negotiate consequences for failure to see the agreement through.
5. If the testing period produces evidence that the conflict is not properly managed or resolved, don't be afraid to go back to the drawing board for revision or development of a new agreement.

Conflict Resolution Conflict Management Agreement

____

____

____

____

____

____

____

____

We honor the resolution, and or management of this agreement by accepting and following each decision as written/agreed above.

If, for any reason, the Resolution, and or Management of this Agreement is not followed or breaks down, we will seek to revise, or develop a new agreement.

Signed:_________________________Date:___________

Signed:_________________________Date:___________

Signed:_________________________Date:___________

CHAPTER 10

Conflict Management, Resolution, and the Power to Forgive

Remember, conflicts are not all manageable or resolvable. As stated earlier in this book, trying to resolve a conflict that's only manageable and attempting to manage a resolvable conflict is like trying to place a square piece in a round hole; it just won't fit. But when you have all the right pieces in the right places, then hope, healing, and forgiveness are available to all who will receive.

I have been blessed with the opportunity to write this book and practice and train others using these skills. In addition, I've encountered my own life experiences. From those experiences, I have learned that not all conflicts will be properly managed or resolved. We will sometimes get it right and other times horribly wrong. Therefore, in this final chapter I would like to empower you with seven (7) valuable truths in which the first six (6) are embedded throughout this book, and number seven (7) I saved for last. I believe these truths are active in every Peacemaking opportunity and important to remember.

1. Confronting the conflict exposes the conflict.
2. When conflict is not all about your needs, you empower yourself to meet the needs of others.
3. To earn trust you must do the hard work.

4. Doing the hard work creates a healthy atmosphere for change.
5. You're empowered to master or manage conflict rather than allow conflict to master or manage you.
6. Courageously exposing conflict provides opportunities to properly manage or resolve conflict.
7. Forgiveness is not just a possibility; it is a reality.

Before diving into the seventh and final truth listed above, let me ask you a very important question. When it comes to conflicts within and with others, would you define yourself as a *Peacemaker* or *Peacekeeper*? I raise this question because it is important for you to understand that the driving force of this book is *Peacemaking*. Writing this book required a detailed review of past training materials I've written, which resulted in me coming across a personal study I did concerning the difference between the words *Peacemaking* and *Peacekeeping*. Between those two words you will find a dramatic difference.

Matthew 5:9 says, "Blessed are the peacemakers, for they shall be called sons of God." Biblically, a *Peacemaker's* ability to make peace reflects God's likeness and glory. So, if *peacemakers* are responsible for making peace, then why did Jesus charge into the temple in Jerusalem (St. John 2:13–17), make a whip, turn over tables, and run those that sold doves out of his Father's house as he said, "Do not make My Father's house a house of merchandise!" Jesus created such a scene because making peace, does not mean there will not be disagreement and, at times, confrontation.

The sixth (6th) valuable truth requires a willingness to courageously expose conflict, because such exposure provides opportunities to properly manage or resolve conflicts within and with others. Exposing conflict is what leads to the seventh (7th) valuable truth which is forgiveness. Forgiveness is more than a possibility; it is a living reality. In St John 2:13-17, Jesus did the hard work by confronting and exposing conflict to properly resolve or manage it. So again, I ask, when it comes to conflicts within and with others, would you define yourself as a *Peacemaker* or *Peacekeeper*? *Peacemakers* not only think about how God makes peace but also about what it requires and demands.

I heard a sermon about the difference between *Peacemakers* and *Peacekeepers* preached by Pastor J.R. Lee of the Freedom Church Pastor Lee said, "The key to peace is to stop keeping it and start making it. Jesus embraced conflict so that we can experience the peace he chose to make for us. Peacekeepers often walk on eggshells and apologize for things they haven't done wrong." I would take the above quote a step further by saying that Peacekeeping often involves a great deal of stuffing. In mental health, stuffing involves constantly swallowing your words and feelings instead of properly expressing them. You keep stuffing and stuffing and stuffing all for the sake of keeping peace while at the same time failing to experience real and lasting peace. As a result, all it takes is for one simple thing to go wrong for you to explode emotionally. Many marriages have failed because of *Peacekeeping*. Many adults have lost touch with who they really are because they are simply trying to keep the peace rather than make peace. This often results in what I call surface-level relation-ships that, for years, have been held together because of children or some other long-term responsibility. Once those responsibilities no longer exist, the marriage often falls apart. The focus of this book is not to teach you how to go along, just to simply get along. No, this book is challenging you to be a *Peacemaker*, not simply a *Peacekeeper*. There's a major difference between the two.

As you get ready to read and explore the seventh (7th) and final truth, it's important that you do so, knowing that your power to for-give in many ways depends upon your decision to either make peace or keep peace.

I saved number seven (7) as this book's closure for many rea-sons. To name a few, let me start by saying that forgiveness isn't always immediate. Depending on the circumstances, forgiveness can take time. Does unforgiveness interfere with and even hinder our relationship with God? Yes, it does, but that doesn't take away the fact that some offenses can be more difficult to forgive than others. I'm not justifying or excusing unforgiveness, but I am shedding light on the fact that for many reasons, some people choose to remain imprisoned by the chains of unforgiveness. Let's explore why such choices are made in this final chapter.

As difficult as it may sometimes be, I believe the power to forgive is embedded in every conflict we face within and with others. Yes, you can forgive the person who wronged you, and you can find the ability to wish a person well when their feelings are not mutual. Forgiveness is possible and can also be your reality, no matter how deep the pain and the hurt. To truly understand this reality, let's begin by understanding what forgiveness isn't. Forgiveness is not forgetting, nor is it merely getting over something or letting it go. How often have you heard people define forgiveness with such insensitivity and brutality? I'm sure more than you care to count.

Try telling a person that was raped or molested to forget the experience or telling a husband that's still healing from the death of his wife to get over it, and a woman or man that's been in an abusive relationship to just let it go. Such insensitivity is not only cruel, but it can also be spiritually, mentally, and emotionally devastating to a person facing conflicts within and with others. The truth is, forgiveness has nothing to do with forgetting, nor is it experienced because you think it's time for a person to either get over it or just let it go. No, it's quite the contrary. Forgiveness is the conscience choice to no longer hold another person's fault against them. When a person injures you, and you can engage and communicate without labeling blame for past mistakes and possess the ability to still wish them well, then that's evidence that forgiveness has become your reality.

There are several reasons why people struggle with forgiveness. Some believe that if they forgive, they justify the offender's behavior, as they are unfairly released from the damage they've done without experiencing real and lasting consequences. Others believe that forgiveness will relinquish control of their pain by bringing an end to their journey at a time when they remain in spiritual, mental, and emotional turmoil. Many fail to realize that forgiveness doesn't justify wrong behavior; it exposes it for what it really is. Forgiveness is not the end of your journey; it is the beginning. Misunderstandings about forgiveness encourage people to hold onto bitterness by refusing to release the offender from the mistakes they've made, which places the person on an endless journey filled with hurt that manifest into anger that develops into a downward cycle that further distances a person's relationship with God and with other people. If you are not careful, the emotional baggage of bitterness and anger will attach itself to your next relationship. It will easily consume every aspect of your life, leaving you a spiritual, emotional, and psychological wreck. Your ability to resolve some conflicts and manage others will help empower you to release the offender and rescue yourself from the bondage of the offense and the self-imposed torture of an unforgiving heart. If unforgiveness is a reality in your heart today, know that God has not and never will give up on your ability to forgive. He will intervene in your space and time and, by His power, move you away from bitterness and place you on a path that leads you to enjoy the freedom, joy, and power to forgive. That's exactly what God did for me. He moved me from a place of bitterness/anger, and now I enjoy the freedom, joy, and power to forgive.

Recent life experiences moved me to take my years of experience as a trainer and write this book. There are many experiences I could share, but the most challenging was the death of my wife. Her death exposed many conflicts within and with others. I felt I had no choice but to confront, manage, resolve, and find healing to the best of my God-given abilities. I know what it means and how it feels to be injured by others. For example, just a few months after my wife's death, one of the deacons of the church I then pastored told me during a pastor/deacons meeting that I needed to get over my wife's death and get on with my life and duties as a pastor. If that wasn't bad enough, it was even more challenging and hurtful to sit there in a God-directed pause as I waited for other deacons to hold that deacon accountable, which never happened. I had to speak up for myself. I also had to deal with private matters between my wife and I that were suddenly made public. As I wrestled with one conflict after another, I had to figure out how to respect my wife's privacy while at the same time confront the many conflicts I faced within and with others. Conflicts like, how do I help my children come to terms with not being able to say goodbye to their stepmother after being told that they would get to visit her on the very day she unexpectedly died?

How do I honor her wishes and find peace at the same time? After experiencing such hurt, and feeling unsupported as a pastor, how do I pick up the pieces, put life back together, and move on? How do I protect my youngest daughter from the cruelties of this world?

For healing to truly take place, I had to let go of *Peacekeeping* and become a *Peacemaker.* I had to do the hard work by confronting and exposing the true nature of the conflict to resolve or properly manage them. As a result, forgiveness is no longer a possibility, for me, forgiveness is my testimony and my reality.

If I could find healing and forgiveness in my heart despite a treacherous journey, so can you. I live by Ephesians 4:32, which says, "And be kind to one another, tenderhearted, forgiving one another, even as God in Christ forgave you."

A new lease on life can be experienced when you confront and expose conflicts within and with others honestly and with courage. As you chart a new course in life that leads to renewed relationships, remember that forgiveness is not just possible, it can be your reality—a reality that will educate and empower you in ways you can't imagine.

Elton Young is a native of Chattanooga, Tennessee. He grew up in the Brainerd Community and was enrolled in public education up until his graduation from Brainerd High School. He became a Christian at the age of twelve, received his calling to preach at the age of sixteen, was officially licensed under the Foundation of Holiness, and was later ordained upon the recommendation and request of the New Monumental Baptist Church under the leadership of the late great Dr. Virgil J. Caldwell. After honorably serving in the United States Marine Corps, he returned home and enrolled at Unity Theological Seminary, where he completed academic studies in educational ministries. After completing his studies at UTS, he enrolled at Christian Bible College and Seminary, where he received his bachelor of arts degree in biblical counseling and psychology and his master of arts degree in Christian counseling and psychology. Postgraduate studies have humbly earned him past licensure in family mediation and certification in relapse prevention counseling. He has served as dean of Christian leadership schools and a Sunday school commentary writer under the Sunday School Publishing Board (SSPB) of the National Baptist Convention USA, Inc.

Seminary studies, mentorships, and other life experiences have thoroughly equipped Elton Young to successfully pastor four churches over the course of his pastoral tenure thus far. Those churches include serving as interim pastor of Shady Grove Missionary Baptist Church, senior pastor of Mount Paran Missionary Baptist Church, and interim pastor of New Monumental Baptist Church. Today, Elton Young is senior pastor of LifePoint, A Transformational Church (2018), and he serves as president of LifeLine Ministries CRS, Inc (2002).

Elton Young is the humble recipient of the Martin Luther King, Jr. Community Service Award, Focus Award, CHA Commissioner Award, and other recognitions. He recognizes his loving family, father in the ministry, the late great doctor Virgil J. Caldwell, and mentor—the late great doctor Cameron Madison Alexander as powerful influencers in his life that helped shape the ministry God has called him to and the man of God he has become.